Be likeminded one to another

Daniel Andersen

ISBN: 978-1-78364-335-6

www.obt.org.uk

THE OPEN BIBLE TRUST
Fordland Mount, Upper Basildon,
Reading, RG8 8LU, UK.

www.obt.org.uk

Be Likeminded:
one to another

Contents

Introduction

Introduction

In this publication I open my heart to thoughts and feelings that have been reached after years of Bible study. Years ago I was a zealous and dogmatic supporter of a certain line of "fundamentalist thinking" and could react with some indignation to those who differed with me. For in differing with me, my feeling was that they were in opposition to God's truth!

I have realized the limitations and fallibilities of the thinking and reasoning processes of all human beings in general and of myself in particular. I have realized the power and grip of paradigms or patterns of thought over our thinking and how they limit and circumscribe not only our thoughts and views, but the very questions we ask and how we seek. Perhaps the best and truest patterns or paradigms of thought or summaries of doctrines on Biblical subjects have yet to be developed. I have written more fully about these in *Bible Study – a personal quest,* also published by the Open Bible Trust.

1.

Be Likeminded: one to another

1. Be Likeminded: one to another

Be of the same mind one toward another. (Romans 12:16)

Now the God of patience and consolation grant you to *be likeminded one toward another* according to Christ Jesus. (Romans 15:5)

Finally, brethren, farewell. Be perfect, be of good comfort, *be of one mind,* live in peace; and the God of love and peace shall be with you. (2 Corinthians 13:11)

Fulfil ye my joy, *that ye be likeminded,* having the same love, being of one accord, of one mind. (Philippians 2:2)

I beseech Euodias, and beseech Syntyche, that they *be of the same mind* in the Lord. (Philippians 4:2)

These Scripture passages all share a common thought: Paul's exhortation to "be of the same mind," or "be likeminded," or "be of one mind." Each of these phrases uses the Greek verb *phroneo.* We may well wonder just what Paul has in mind in these and similar passages. They apparently make a strong appeal for uniformity. But what kind of uniformity? Does Paul wish everyone to think the same things and in the same way? Is he exhorting believers to subscribe to a uniform set of *articles of faith,* to produce what we might call a *doctrinal accord?* Is it an appeal to embrace a codified set of statements, an early form of *orthodoxy?*

2.
Stewards of the Mysteries (Secrets) of God

2. Steward of the Mysteries (Secrets) of God

I'll confess that for many years this is just what I thought Paul was urging. After all, he was steward of the most profound "secrets of God," one who was an apostle (a commissioned one) of Christ Jesus. He could speak on behalf of Christ. Could he not urge upon all God's people a unanimity of doctrine? Could he not call upon all believers in Christ to submit to a divinely produced creed, to accept an authoritative summary of the essential points that constitute the Christian faith?

For the sake of discussion, let's assume that this is what Paul had in mind, that he was exhorting to a unanimity of thought in regard to those things "most surely to be believed." If he sought such accord in his day when he ministered Christ, what about our day, almost 2,000 years later? We do not have Paul (or any other apostle) in our midst to dispense to us these *essential points of the Christian faith*. We do not have anyone divinely commissioned to give us directly a doctrinal summary of God's truth. But it is claimed, we have Paul's writings (and more, the set of writings we call the New Testament). And so it behooves us to study, to search, to seek to understand and properly interpret these writings. Would that this were sufficient to produce a unanimity, a oneness, an accord among all believers in Christ! Sad to say, Christendom is characterized by factiousness, fragmentation, and divisiveness rather than by agreement, accord, and unanimity. Shall we strive to attain a common set of doctrines, to agree on a particular set of Biblical articles of faith, to reach one mind and be of total accord? If so, whose mind shall it be? Mine, yours, or someone else's? What set of doctrines shall all commonly embrace? Mine, yours, or someone else's?

3.
The legacy of
orthodoxy

3. The legacy of orthodoxy

Dogmatic adherence to a particular creed or *confession* as the basis for unity will produce unity only for the adherents to that particular system. And this, in practice, appears to be about the only basis for unity that is generally recognized. We suffer from what I call the "legacy of orthodoxy," the idea that one must submit to a particular set of dogmatically proclaimed *orthodox* beliefs to be a Christian, or to be a member of some church, or to have fellowship with other Christians.

We observe dogmatism in so many human enterprises, in philosophy, in religion, in politics. It appears to be a universal human trait to be zealously engaged in supporting dogmatically held ideas. In world affairs we see the results of such dogmatism: fanatical zeal in the support of a particular cause. And so often it leads to more than fragmentation and division; it leads to bloodshed. Paul himself knew intimately what such zealousness could produce. It was a trait which once characterized himself, but which he ultimately discarded, casting it upon the refuse heap of worthless works of the flesh.

It appears totally impossible for Christians to experience a real unity if it is to be based upon a set of articles of faith or system of doctrines. If this is what Paul was urging, we'd have to say it may have been possible in his day, but it is certainly not possible in our day. Many seek to rise above petty differences and say that they will have fellowship with any who simply agree on *the fundamentals*.

A petty difference might be whether grape juice or wine should be used in the communion service. Or whether water baptism should be observed by immersion or by sprinkling. But what about communion and water baptism themselves? Are they in the list of *fundamentals*? There are sincere believers in Christ who do not observe these ceremonies and do not consider them as in the will of God for His people today. Would all who hold various points of view on these matters have fellowship with those who differ with them?

Again, most Christians embrace the concept of a Triune Godhead, a Trinity of persons: God the Father, God the Son, and God the Holy Spirit. To many, the confession of being a Christian is practically the same as being a Trinitarian. And yet there are many sincere and serious believers in Christ who do not embrace the concept of a Trinity of Persons in the Godhead. Are they to be branded as heretics? This would certainly be a *fundamental* upon which there is disagreement. Must those holding one view reject fellowship with those holding others? If so, why?

4.
What basis for accord?

4. What basis for accord?

Some will reply, "Can two walk together, except they be agreed?" (Amos 3:3). Yes, but agreed on what? A topic or activity of mutual interest can bring harmony and agreement between people of the greatest diversity of views. That's why people form clubs and associations of all kinds. Have you noticed how friendly people are in a campground visiting and sharing experiences? Or in a hiking club or biking club or health club, etc.? People from tremendously different points of view on many things can get along in great harmony when sharing something of common interest.

So what should be the basis for harmony, for agreement among believers in Christ? Should it be concepts of the Godhead, some of the most complex and subtle theological doctrines that have ever been developed? What if a person, by diligent, honest searching and study, finds it necessary to change views on the nature of the

Godhead? Is this one now to be expelled from fellowship? Even from that of one's own family?

Isn't this just what we observe in Christendom? There is a proliferation of groups, denominations, sects, large and small, some respected and venerated, some of long standing and some of recent origin. They are organized around some doctrinal basis or creed or *confession*. The concepts of *orthodoxy* and *heresy* become a matter of concern, but these are not easy to define and they vary in range and scope. Is it *orthodox* to believe the dead are conscious in heaven or hell, but *heresy* to believe the dead "sleep in the dust of the earth" awaiting resurrection (Daniel 12:2)? Is it *orthodox* to accept the Trinity, but *heresy* to accept the Oneness concept? (This is not to imply that these are the only options.) Is it *orthodox* to claim Christ is the eternal Son of God but *heresy* to understand that the Son of God came into being by conception and birth?

How many reach their ideas of what is *orthodox* by their own personal diligent study of the Bible and coming to their own private conclusions?

Very few, I'm sure. Most simply *subscribe* to a system that, for one reason or another, they are persuaded is *orthodox*. It could be argued that it would be impossible for everyone to reach the *orthodox faith* if left to seek and study and find it for themselves. I agree. And for precisely that reason we ought to dismiss the concept of *orthodoxy* and find a totally different basis for fellowship than agreement on a set of doctrines or a creed or a *confession*.

5.

Paul's day and our day

5. Paul's day and our day

Let's continue, for the sake of discussion, to suppose Paul was urging believers to the doctrinal kind of unity we have been describing. As mentioned earlier, perhaps it could work in his day, but not in ours. Assuming this, we must inquire as to what happened later on. We have the answer in what is generally considered Paul's last letter:

> And the things that thou has heard of me among many witnesses, the same commit thou to faithful men, who shall be able to teach others also. (2 Timothy 2:2)

It would be wonderful if we could find a direct line of this commitment to faithful men from Paul's day to our own! But we seek it in vain. And we must admit that this produces a totally different situation from having Paul himself among us. Church historians have indicated that for quite an extended period there was a beautiful freedom of thought and inquiry. People would meet and freely discuss ideas about the nature of the Godhead and other profound topics of the Scriptures, as freely as we today meet and talk about the weather. There was no fear of embracing *heresy*.

As time went on there developed a crystallization along particular doctrinal lines. Systematic theologies began to be produced. Prominent church *bishops* attracted followings. Divisions along doctrinal lines developed. And then, to me, the most tragic event of all took place. Constantine the Great used Christianity to consolidate his power, nominally making the Roman Empire a *Christian Empire*. He convened the Council of Nicaea in 325 A.D., demanding that it unify the Christian Church so that he could more effectively administer the affairs of the empire.

This council, beset by factions and strife, finally produced what is called the *Nicene Creed*. It was declared to be the *orthodox faith*. All must submit to it or face the threat of persecution, loss of property, loss of family, even loss of life, and, of course, loss of salvation. No longer was there healthy inquiry and freedom of discussion. This was replaced by fear and submission to authority.

Confessedly, church bishops and officials who, with the backing of the civil government, demanded submission by the populace, did not even themselves understand the intricacies and subtleties of the doctrinal system of faith they now enforced. Splits and antagonisms developed over the interpretation or meaning of a single word. Sometimes a word used to express a theological concept was not a word in the Bible itself.

In the 4th century, insistence upon a particular interpretation of one such word, used to describe the Person of Christ, "let loose a fury among mankind that has rarely been paralleled. Millions suffered violence or death in the pursuant wars and persecutions. Hundreds of bishops were exiled or murdered at the command of other bishops who, when the tide turned, visited the same treatment upon their rivals." Those of opposing views "alike sought to use the secular arm to terrify and assassinate their opponents, and to seize their congregations, churches, and revenues by force." (*The religion of the Occident*, by Martin A. Larson, Littlefield, Adams & Co., 1961, p. 572).

We wonder how individual and personal faith in Christ as one's own personal Saviour would be possible under such conditions. We might well wonder why we today should esteem as *orthodox* the deliberations of church officials who were so obviously manipulated. They produced a system that, by binding together a culturally diverse population resulted in the aggrandizement of power both by a Roman Emperor and by those same church officials. Let us be ever so grateful for the freedom we enjoy, freedom to investigate and examine and question, and to have personal faith according to our individual understanding in a living One, the One Who died and rose again on our behalf!

So, for the sake of discussion, we'd say that Paul could be dogmatic but we cannot be. He could urge agreement on a set of dogmatically declared articles of faith, but we cannot. We should welcome free and open discussion. We should welcome healthy and sincere inquiry. We should be free to work through to our own conclusions on all Scriptural topics and themes. Yes, I believe we should!

6.
What was in Paul's mind?

6. What was in Paul's mind?

But we must examine the possibility that Paul had something totally different in mind from what we have so far considered here. Do Paul's writings convey the impression that he imposed a codified set of doctrines upon those whom he ministered? That he had a systematically organized creed to which people were to be subjected? Does he not rather appeal to people to believe God's truth, to receive the word of Christ in faith?

Read again such passages as 1 Thessalonians 1 and Colossians 1 and try to get the feeling of Paul's ministry: his love, his prayers, and his concern for these believers. He tells the Colossians that as they received Christ Jesus the Lord, so they should walk in Him; having been rooted in Him, they should continue to grow up in Him (2:6, 7). This hardly suggests being subjected to a detailed system of thought. It rather suggests a dynamic, living faith that reaches out and embraces Christ in a most personal, intimate manner. The concept of growth implies development and change and adjustment. We were not born with the truth. The truth must be obtained. This is not an effortless task. It requires diligence and effort. And it must become a lifetime quest, never a total or absolute attainment. Psalm 119:105 describes our situation as walking along a path, with God's Word to give light, showing us where to place our feet, step by step.

7.

The verb

phroneo:

"to be

likeminded"

7. The verb *phroneo*: "to be likeminded"

But now we must come to grips with the Greek verb *phroneo* that Paul used in each of the verses quoted at the start of this publication. It comes from the root *phren* which literally means the "diaphragm" or "midriff". But the Greek, as well as many languages, often used such words to describe something beyond literal bodily organs. For instance, think of the literal and many figurative uses of the word "heart."

The Greek word *splagchna* (from *spleen*, from which we obtain "spleen") literally means the "intestines" and is most often translated "bowels" in the *King James Version*. But it can describe inward and tender affection and compassion, as is clearly indicated in the contexts in which it is used. In a similar manner the word *phren*, and the family of words based upon it, came to have connotations far beyond that of the "midriff" or "diaphragm". Look up the words *phrenic* and *phrenology* in a dictionary that indicates the origins of words.

The Greek word *phren*, diaphragm, will be indicated as the origin, but phrenology is the study of the conformation of the skull as indicative of mental faculties.

The Greeks connected the diaphragm with the mind, but neither in the sense of pure reasoning nor in the exercise of the mental faculties in taking thought or thinking something through. It was rather considered the source of, or associated with, sympathy, with feelings of a sensitive nature. So *phroneo* carries with it emotional overtones. It includes the idea of a disposition, an attitude, a leaning, or inclination.

The *Analytical Greek Lexicon* (Harper and Brothers, New York) includes under it the following: "to entertain sentiments or inclinations of a specific kind." Thayer's Lexicon includes the definition "to feel, to think." How often we speak of our mental feelings or inclinations about things. Note how often we say "I feel…" about a matter as an indication of our attitude or disposition or inclination about it. These remarks indicate the richness and flexibility of words in various languages.

8.
Interpersonal relationships

8. Interpersonal relationships

Let's now examine the use of *phroneo* in a few passages.

> For I say through the favour which hath been given me unto everyone who is among you, not to think of himself more highly (*huperphroneo*) than he ought to think (*phroneo*), but so to think (*phroneo*) as to think soberly (*sophroneo*) – as unto each one God hath dealt a measure of faith. (Romans 12:3, *Rotherham*)

Here we have two occurrences of the word *phroneo* and two occurrences of compoundings of the word. The meaning is clear: "Don't be highminded about yourself above what you ought to be minded. Don't think too highly, too loftily about self, with overtones of superiority. Don't have a high and mighty attitude. Don't display a haughty attitude." Reading the context of this verse indicates that the matter of relationships among the Roman Christians is Paul's subject and concern. In this important matter he desires the appropriate attitude or inclination or sentiment to be exhibited by each to the other.

> Be of the same mind (*phroneo*) one toward another. Mind not (*phroneo*) high things, but condescend to men of low estate. Be not wise (*phronimos*, adjective form of *phroneo*) in your own conceits. (Romans 12:16)

Read the entire beautiful context of this verse. It is so obvious that Paul is dealing with *attitudes* to be displayed by people in their relationships with one another. He urges them to be intimately united in the acceptance of one another, to be condescending, to be open, outgoing, warm, concerned and compassionate in personal matters.

9.
Christ:
the focus and
the pattern

9. Christ: the focus and the pattern

> Now the God of patience and consolation grant you to be likeminded [literally, to mind (*phroneo*) the same thing] one toward another according to Christ Jesus (Romans 15:5)

Again, the context must be studied to appreciate Paul's thoughts. He appeals to these believers not simply to live to please themselves, but to live to please others, to live for the good of others, edifying and building them up in the faith. Christ didn't live to please Himself and a person who allows self to suffer the reproaches directed at another isn't living for self. The quoted Scripture is for direct application and instruction, bringing endurance and encouragement.

In verse 5 Paul prays that the God of that endurance and encouragement would grant them the same mind Christ displayed. This is in order that, with one accord and one mouth, they might glorify the God and Father of our Lord Jesus Christ. And so, to pull it all together (v7), *they ought to receive one another in the same manner and spirit that Christ received them.* And this would be to the glory of God!

It is fascinating to read this passage in different translations to see how various translators attempt to express Paul's thoughts in English. Here is Moffatt's rendering of verses 5 and 6.

> May the God who inspires steadfastness and encouragement grant you such harmony with one another, after Christ Jesus, that you may unite in a chorus of praise and glory to the God and Father of our Lord Jesus Christ!

Here is Phillips' rendering of verses 5-7.

> May ... God ... give you a mind united toward one another because of your common loyalty to Jesus Christ. And then, as one man, you will sing from the heart the praises of God the Father of our Lord Jesus

Christ. So open your hearts to one another as Christ has opened his heart to you, and God will be glorified.

No passage could indicate more clearly the importance to God of how His people relate to one another and what their attitudes should be to one another.

Christ Himself is the model and motivation. He didn't live to please Himself. He receives all that come to Him without discriminating, without qualifications, and without presenting a list of prerequisites.

The Roman Christians must have been a very mixed group of people with a variety of social, cultural and religious backgrounds. Many, perhaps most, were Israelites dispersed from their homeland, some of whom may have become indifferent to their ancient heritage under the Law of Moses. Some may have sought to remain loyal to that heritage in whatever way they could.

Others were likely Italians with backgrounds in ancient Roman religions. Still others may have come from various ethnic groups in the civilized world of the day. Some had high social status, some low. Some were wealthy, some poor. Some were highly educated, some uneducated. Christ received them all. Thus they should receive one another. There should be no discrimination, no overriding concern about status, genealogy, family background, roots, intellectual or mental level, capabilities, financial status, educational background, religious background, etc..

So it is clear that Paul is dealing with attitudes, with feelings, with inclinations. He is not speaking of subscribing to a codified set of doctrinal statements, of being *indoctrinated* into a creed or confession. He appeals for the unity of a warm, loving, compassionate reception of one another as Christ received them. Their acceptance of one another should transcend every kind of distinction that would tend to cause division and differences among them. Paul clearly indicates that Christ is the focus, the model, the pattern. And, wonder of wonders, the glory of God is in it!

Should we not apply Paul's exhortation to ourselves today? Should we not receive to ourselves in every way possible all those whom He has received, all who have *named the name of Christ*? Should we not remove all prerequisites and qualifications and embrace into our fellowship all who have committed themselves to Him? And isn't that the basis for unity, for fellowship: *the Person of Christ Himself*? Shall we make demands that He does not make? Shall we erect barriers that He would not raise? Shall we exclude where He receives? Shall we demand agreement on subtle and complex theological notions when He looks for simple faith?

Going on to another occurrence:

> When I was a child, I spake as a child, I understood (*phroneo*) as a child, I thought as a child, but when I became a man, I put away childish things. (1 Corinthians 13:11)

Here is Rotherham's translation of this verse.

When I was a child I used to speak as a child, to prefer (*phroneo*) as a child, to reason as a child: now I have become a man I have laid aside the things of the child!

It seems plain that the Greek word we are investigating, *phroneo*, does not here refer to what we might call intellectual concerns. It describes what we might call "child-mindedness" and speaks of the attitude, preferences, disposition, and understanding that is typical of a child. When maturity comes, these things, along with manner of speaking and manner of reasoning, change to those characteristics of adulthood.

10.
The mind of Christ:
the ultimate pattern

10. The mind of Christ: the ultimate pattern

Let this mind (*phroneo*) be in you, which was also in Christ Jesus. (Philippians 2:5)

This exhortation is in a context which clearly indicates Paul's concern for the interactions and interrelationships of these believers amongst themselves. He is concerned that their fellowship be characterized by love and harmony, by compassion and accord, without strife or vainglory.

Each should humbly esteem the other as above or better than self. Rather than living in a self-centered manner, thinking only of oneself and one's own needs and affairs, each should be considering the welfare and the needs of others. Each one's attitude or disposition or *leaning* should be the same as was displayed by Christ. So again Christ is the example of the way Christians should behave amongst themselves. Rather than seeking His own welfare, rather than seeking to please Himself, He displayed an entirely different attitude. He emptied Himself. He humbled Himself.

It is certainly true that Philippians 2:5-11 speaks volumes about what we call *Christology*, the study of the Person and the nature of the Lord Jesus Christ. But we should not lose sight of Paul's main point here. It is not his purpose to give a doctrinal development of the nature of the Godhead, but to extend the exhortations of verses 1-4, giving strength and focus to them. Christ is the supreme example of condescension of one who, instead of pursuing a path of grasping and self-seeking, pursued the path of humility and self-abnegation. He stooped. He emptied Himself. He left the *morphe theos* (form of God) and took upon Himself *a morphe doulou* (form of a bondslave).

I particularly enjoy Phillips' rendering of verses 1-5 and include it here. Notice that the word *phroneo* also occurs twice in verse 2 ("be likeminded" and "of one mind," *KJV*).

> Now if your experience of Christ's encouragement and love means anything to you, if you have known something of the fellowship of his Spirit, and all that it means in kindness and deep sympathy, do make my best hopes for you come true! Live together in harmony (*phroneo*), live together in love, as though you had only one mind (*phroneo*) and one spirit between you. Never act from motives of rivalry or personal vanity, but in humility think more of one another than you do of yourselves. None of you should think only of his own affairs, but each should learn to see things from other people's point of view. Let Christ Jesus be your example as to what your attitude (*phroneo*) should be.

Now on to the next reference to be examined.

> But I rejoiced in the Lord greatly, that now at last your care (*phroneo*) of me hath flourished again; wherein ye were also

careful (*phroneo*), but ye lacked opportunity. (Philippians 4:10)

This clearly shows that the word we are investigating does not refer to mind in the sense of reasoning or grasping matters of intellectual content, but rather refers to mind in the sense of attitude or leaning or disposition. The Philippians once had a "mindedness" concerning Paul which was sensitive, concerned, and compassionate. Paul rejoiced that they were once again of this "mind" concerning him and his state. Many translators follow the *King James* Version and use the words "care" and "caring" here. We give Philips' translation to further indicate the sense of this word.

> It has been a great joy to me that after all this time you have shown such interest (*phroneo*) in my welfare. I don't mean that you had forgotten me, but up till now you had no opportunity of expressing your concern (*phroneo*).

11.
Things above: things on the earth

11. Things above: things on the earth

Here is another familiar verse where the Greek work *phroneo* is used.

> Set your affection (*phroneo*) on things above, not on things on the earth. (Colossians 3:2)

The ideas of affection, leaning, disposition, attitude that we have discussed as the meaning of *phroneo*, are clearly indicated here. Some translators simply render it, "Mind (*phroneo*) the things above, not the things on the earth." Phillips, with his characteristic touch, renders it:

> Give your heart (*phroneo*) to the heavenly things, not to the passing things of earth.

We should ask just what Paul meant by "the things above" and "the things on the earth" in this passage. I can hardly believe this phrase describes material objects or things in a physical sense. He has just spoken of the Risen Christ in His place of glory at the right hand of God. Would not "the things above" then be those truths, those thoughts, which concern the glories of Christ in His resurrection life wherein He "lives unto God," as Paul puts it in Romans 6:10?

And perhaps the "things on the earth" refers to those legalisms so characteristic of so many religious systems. Paul had just queried (2:20-22), "… if ye are dead with Christ … why, as though living in the world, are ye subject to ordinances (Greek, *dogmatizo*) … after the commandments and doctrines of men?" So perhaps the "things on the earth" of 3:2 is a reference back to all those ritualistic rules and regulations that cater to fleshly pride, to the many things discussed in 2:16-23 (or perhaps 2:8-23). Such things direct attention away from the Person of Christ and His work and His glory.

The moral dimension must also be included here, for in 3:5 Paul speaks directly of a set of familiar vices as members which are "upon the earth" (same phrase as in 3:2) and which are to be placed in the state of death. The instruction to "mortify therefore" in 3:5 is more clearly rendered "put to death." Here is Moffatt's translation of Colossians 3:5-6.

> So put to death those members that are on earth: sexual vice, impurity, appetite, evil desire, and lust (which is as bad as idolatry), things which bring down God's anger on the sons of disobedience.

This appeals to me as a practical application of Paul's exhortation in Romans 6:11 to "reckon yourselves to be dead indeed unto sin … in Christ Jesus our Lord." It is not a "dying daily" or "crucifying self daily" as some exhort. It is an accounting or reckoning that is done once for all and is to be considered accomplished. Then these vices can have no more influence than something or someone that is dead. This thought fits Paul's ongoing exhortation in the context: "you have put off the old man with his deeds and have put on the new man which is renewed in knowledge according to the image of the One Who created him" (Colossians 3:9-10).

In close association with the thoughts from Colossians 3 is Philippians 3:19 where Paul describes some who "mind (phroneo) earthly things." Their mindedness, their disposition, their leaning, is toward self-indulgence and immorality, as Paul makes clear in the context. Here is the *New English* Bible rendering of Philippians 3:17-20.

> Agree together, my friends, to follow my example. You have us for a model; watch those whose way of life conforms to it. For, as I have often told you, and now tell you with tears in my eyes, there are many whose way of life makes them enemies of the cross of Christ. They are heading for destruction, appetite is their god, and they glory in their shame. Their minds are set (*phroneo*) on earthly things. We, by contrast, are citizens of heaven, and from heaven we expect our deliverer to come, the Lord Jesus Christ.

Clearly the word we are investigating has to do with attitude or disposition, and with thoughts of an emotional nature, not purely intellectual. Wherever this word occurs, it appears to speak of the *mind-set,* disposition or inclination.

12.
What can we conclude?

12. What can we conclude?

I think we can form certain conclusions as to the kind of unity, the kind of likemindedness, that Paul was urging and that he so long for among believers in Christ. It was a unity of inclination and attitude, of feelings and affection. It was a unity that centered in the Person of Christ, not in *Christology*. Of course the study of the Person of Christ is of deep concern to every believer in Him, but I distinguish between the study of the Person of Christ and the act of reaching out in simple faith and commitment to Him. A study can be bookish. It uses facts and information that are looked up and put together in some kind of meaningful, systematic, and consistent form. I do not make light of this, it is certainly important.

Further, the act of simple faith in Christ has as its basis information we find written or hear spoken, and which we grasp with the use of some mental effort. But what is that information? It is that this

One, by experiencing intense personal suffering and death, has done a work for God on our behalf that clears us from any taint of sin or offence. And upon the accomplishment of that work He was raised in triumph from the dead! So faith reaches out to One Who lives, a Living Person, and makes a personal commitment to Him for care and safe-keeping!

This is something so vital, so dynamic, and so intimately personal. The believer in Christ has related self to a living Saviour. There are no barriers, no prerequisites, no exams to pass, no IQ level to attain, no doctrinal qualifications, no fee to pay. And no other person, high or low, and no institution, however large or small, dare intrude here and make a judgment or introduce a restriction or demand.

Many there are who have "named the Name of Christ" as the One they are depending on to relate themselves properly to God and to Whom they have committed themselves for their eternal well-being. They are all over the earth. They are to be found in a great proliferation of religious denominations or in no denomination at all. Most have subscribed to a creed or catechism or confession and have been taught that this is the basis for Christian fellowship and harmony, or even salvation! The creed or catechism or confession enables them to recognize what is correct or orthodox, as distinct from what is error or heresy. But on this basis, what is *orthodox* to one is *error or heresy* to another. The fragmentation and division which we see is bound to be the result.

13.
One in Christ

13. One in Christ

Paul insists that all believers are "one in Christ." Would that all believers might express the reality of that oneness in their lives and conduct as they relate to other believers. How can any who have forgiveness in Christ reject any others who have forgiveness in Christ? How can any who have "died with Christ" reject any others who have died with Him? How can any whom Christ loves and accepts not love, in deed as well as in word, others whom Christ loves and accepts?

It is the Person of Christ that is the focus, the centre, the basis for unity. We shall ever grow in Him. We shall ever learn more of the "things concerning Himself." We shall doubtless change and should ever seek to correct our understanding concerning Himself, to say nothing of the many other topics throughout the Bible. But that knowledge and understanding should not and *must not* be the basis for unity or accord. No two people can possibly agree on everything!

Believers in Christ come from a diversity of cultural and ethnic backgrounds, a diversity of religious thought, a diversity of understanding and grasp of the Bible. *But it is Christ they all have in common!*

It is the Person of the Saviour and His acceptance of all who come to Him that must be the basis for accord. Differences should be discussed in an atmosphere of love and respect, seeking to understand the other's point of view, and always seeking to edify or build up one another in the faith in Christ.

When the person of Christ is the object of faith and affection, one cannot become overly upset concerning differences in interpretation or differences in understanding about major or minor Bible topics and doctrines. For me to insist that everyone agree with me might be a subtle form of self-justification, the feeling that I must be right. To be argumentative, to be contentious about differences, to continually grind an axe about a particular point of view could be the sowing of discord. Sowing of discord is listed among the things the Lord hates (Proverbs 6:16-19).

Paul never instructed the dismissal of a person for having honest differences of understanding. He may even have urged a venturesome spirit in the consideration of various thoughts that might possibly speak for God or convey divine truth, i.e. "prophecies". A loose paraphrase of 1 Thessalonians 5:19-21 could be as follows: "Don't stifle the spirit (of inquiry or investigation). Don't despise prophetic utterances. Rather bring them all to the test and retain what is good in them."

14.

A man that is an heretic ... reject!

14. A man that is an heretic ... reject!

The Greek words for "heretic" and "heresy" do not have the connotations that we, due to our legacy of orthodoxy, attach to these English words today. The Greek words have to do with factiousness and contentiousness, the raising of dissension and the sowing of discord. Thus Paul's admonition in Titus 3:10 is usually misunderstood and has been used as the basis for dismissing or excommunicating persons with different points of view or differing beliefs. Rather Paul was talking about one who is constantly argumentative and contentious. Here is the *New International Version's* rendering of this verse.

> Warn a divisive (Greek, *hairetikon*) person once, and then warn him a second time. After that, have nothing to do with him.

Such a person has not grasped the real meaning of that "likemindedness one toward another according to Christ Jesus." Such a person does not appreciate that a personal relationship to the Living Saviour is the dynamic and basis for fellowship and harmony with fellow believers.

Let us examine ourselves. Let us search our hearts. Let us dismiss any attitude of thinking less of others who do not have precisely the same views we have. Let us dismiss any feeling of haughtiness in regard to others who have named the name of Christ. Let us never belittle another who has embraced the same Lord as Saviour. Christians should come to the place where they can share their thoughts and convictions regarding the Scriptures without fear of recrimination or ridicule or ostracism.

The Bible is a fast storehouse or treasury with so much to sift through, ponder, discover, and enjoy. Each one should experience the freedom to engage in the quest for its truths without the strait jacket of codified systems of thought to hinder or restrict one's thinking, contemplation and assimilation of its contents. Christ has purchased perfect freedom for His own. This includes freedom from the restrictions of institutionalized thought and religious systems. He has purchased freedom for each believer to enjoy Himself without barrier and hindrance. Let us stand fast in that liberty wherewith He has made us free.

Appendix 1.
In anticipation
of certain
objections

Appendix 1:
In anticipation of certain objections

Do we not read in the Bible of contending earnestly "for the faith which was once (i.e., once and for all) delivered unto the saints" (Jude 3)? Does not Paul speak of having "kept the faith" (2 Timothy 4:7)? Doesn't he admonish Timothy to "fight the good fight of faith" (1 Timothy 6:12)? And doesn't he warn that "some shall depart from the faith" (1 Timothy 4:1)?

Don't these passages, and many like them, speak of being loyal to and steadfast in something very specific, in certain clearly identifiable truths? Yes, they certainly do! But I challenge anyone to show that these exhortations describe a steadfastness in relation to such codified statements of faith as the Apostles' Creed, the Nicene Creed, the Augsburg Confession, or the Westminster Catechism. (This doesn't necessarily imply that I consider these erroneous. They are simply typical of systematic doctrinal statements that people subscribe to and which then limit their thinking and determine the boundaries of their faith. There are no substantial reasons beyond the veneration of age, their widespread influence, and the respect generated by tradition, to consider them as complete, correct, and scriptural summaries of things "most surely to be believed.")

It is my conviction that *faith in Christ* is not complicated by subtle and complex theological concepts. It is a simple reaching out to Him in dependence upon Him and commitment to Him for His care and keeping in all things related to God. It is based upon simple historical truths to which the New Testament writers were witnesses and concerning which they wrote. These are that Christ died and was raised again from the dead. And, most importantly, that that death was in the character of an offering and sacrifice to God on behalf of human beings. By His death a work was completed which delivers me from the guilt and penalty of personal sin. Further, in His being raised from the dead, a work was accomplished by which I have ultimate deliverance from the very consequence of sin, namely death, that has come as a malady upon the human race. One way to summarize this in simple terms is to say that humanity has need in relation to God and that Christ is the answer to that need. So I come to Christ in simple faith and lay hold of Him as the One sufficient for my personal need.

It is a simple linguistic device to speak of the *act* of believing as "faith", and the *declaration* ("report," "word," see Romans 10:16, 17) concerning Christ, which is the basis for that act of believing, as "the faith" ("the belief"). This does not make the transaction complicated and fraught with entanglements. To illustrate, imagine the following dialogue as the result of a "hearing" or "report" concerning the weather:

> "I *believe* tomorrow will be sunny and warm."
> "Is your *belief* strong enough to plan a picnic?"
> "True to this *belief,* I've arranged for a day at the beach."

It is in this manner that the act of having faith (believing) in Christ can be called *the faith*.

Further, the substance of that which is declared concerning Christ, which produces that act of faith (the acts of believing), can also be called *the faith*. If this thought is associated with such verses as those quoted at the beginning of this appendix, one can see that there are no complications about the matter of simple faith. And there is no contradiction with Paul's thoughts as expressed in this entire presentation.

Appendix 2.

A concordant listing of all the occurrences of the Greek word *phroneo* in the New Testament

Appendix 2:

A concordant listing of all occurrences of the Greek word *phroneo* in the New Testament.

The words translated from *phroneo* are in italics. The reader is urged to read the context or setting of each reference to see if the ideas of mindedness, attitude, feeling, inclination, disposition, fit each occurrence.

Matthew 16:23	*Thou savourest* not the things that be of God.
Mark 8:33	*Thou savourest* not the things that be of God.
Acts 28:22	We desire to hear of thee what *thou thinkest.*
Romans 8:5	They that are after the flesh *do mind* the things of the flesh
Romans 12:3	Not to think of himself more highly than he ought *to think;* but *to think* soberly [literally, not to be high-minded (*huperphroneo*) above what

	one ought to be minded (*phroneo*); but to be minded (*phroneo*) so as to be sober-minded (*sophroneo*)].
Romans 12:16	*Be of the* same *mind* one toward another. *Mind* not high things.
Romans 14:6	He that *regardeth* the day, *regardeth* it unto the Lord; and he that *regardeth* not the day, to the Lord he doth not *regard* it.
Romans 15:5	Grant you *to be* like *minded* one toward another.
1 Corinthians 4:6	Not *to think* of men above that which is written.
1 Corinthians 13:11	*I understood* as a child.
2 Corinthians 13:11	*Be* of one *mind* (literally, *mind* the same thing).
Galatians 5:10	That *ye will be* none otherwise *minded.*
Philippians 1:7	It is meet for me *to think* this of you all.

Philippians 2:2	That ye be *likeminded* ... being of one accord, of one *mind* (literally, the one thing *minding*).
Philippians 2:5	Let this *mind* be in you.
Philippians 3:15	As many as be perfect, be thus *minded;* and if in any thing ye be otherwise *minded.*
Philippians 3:16	Let us *mind* the same thing.
Philippians 3:19	Who *mind* earthly things.
Philippians 4:2	That they be of the same *mind* in the Lord.
Philippians 4:10	Your *care* of me hath flourished again; wherein ye were also *careful.*
Colossians 3:2	*Set* your *affection* on things above.

Notice how many times Paul uses the word *phroneo* in his letter to the Philippians! It must indicate something of the character of this epistle, recalling that this word indicates thoughts of feeling, of emotion, of a sensitive nature. Reading these passages in newer translations and noting the variety of ways the translators render this verb will verify the suggestions about its meaning that have been discussed here.

In this publication, the author opens his heart to his readers confessing that, in the past, he would have reacted with some indignation to those who differed with him doctrinally. However, his continual study of the Scriptures over many years has led him to conclude that, even though certain doctrines may be of supreme importance to him, they should not obscure the one basic fact that all who believe Jesus died for their sins have been accepted by the Lord. That being the case, it becomes Christians of all persuasions to accept whosoever the Savior accepts.

Belief in Christ is the basis of Christian unity, and when Paul exhorts believers to be "likeminded one to another" he is not entreating them to comply with the same code or creed, or to conform to the same confession or catechism. Rather he is appealing to them to accept each other as equals; to accept others as Christ, Himself, accepts them.

———————————

About the Author

Daniel Andersen was born in Berlin, New Jersey, USA in 1925 and raised in Jamestown, New York. He studied at Harvard University, Union College, Dallas Seminary, Houghton College, Columbia University and Michigan State University. He was a Professor of Physics at Grand Valley State University and lived with his wife near Grand Rapids, Michigan, USA.

Also by
Daniel Andersen

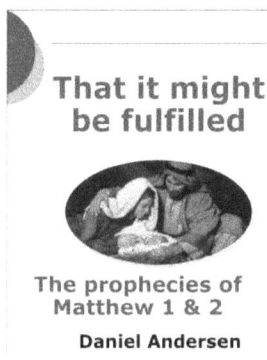

**Be
Likeminded**

one to another

Daniel Andersen

**Be reconciled
to God**

**A perspective on
biblical evangelism**

Daniel Andersen

**Bible
Study**

A personal quest

Daniel Andersen

**That it might
be fulfilled**

**The prophecies of
Matthew 1 & 2**

Daniel Andersen

For details of the above please visit
www.obt.org.uk

They can be ordered from that website.

They are available as eBooks from Amazon and
Apple and as KDP paperback from Amazon.

Free sample

For a free sample of
The Open Bible Trust's magazine Search,
please visit

www.obt.org.uk/search

or email

admin@obt.org.uk

About this book

Be likeminded: one to another

In the Bible we read such things as:

- *Be of the same mind* one toward another. (Romans 12:16)
- Now the God of patience and consolation grant you to *be likeminded one toward another* according to Christ Jesus. (Romans 15:5)
- Finally, brethren, farewell. Be perfect, be of good comfort, *be of one mind,* live in peace; and the God of love and peace shall be with you. (2 Corinthians 13:11)
- Fulfil ye my joy, *that ye be likeminded,* having the same love, being of one accord, of one mind. (Philippians 2:2)
- I beseech Euodias, and beseech Syntyche, that they *be of the same mind* in the Lord. (Philippians 4:2)

What does it mean to be 'likeminded' or to be of 'one mind' or the 'same mind'?

And who are we to be 'likeminded' with?

Publications of The Open Bible Trust must be in accordance with its evangelical, fundamental and dispensational basis. However, beyond this minimum, writers are free to express whatever beliefs they may have as their own understanding, provided that the aim in so doing is to further the object of The Open Bible Trust. A copy of the doctrinal basis is available at

www.obt.org.uk/doctrinal-basis

or from:

THE OPEN BIBLE TRUST
Fordland Mount, Upper Basildon,
Reading, RG8 8LU, GB

www.ingramcontent.com/pod-product-compliance
Lightning Source LLC
Chambersburg PA
CBHW070547030426
42337CB00016B/2388